GRANDMA'S KEEPSAKE

Memory Journal

whitestar

PHOTO

A Story to Be Told...

A grandmother is a fundamental reference point during childhood, and a pivotal figure in the life of every child, offering loving attention, toys and immeasurable amounts of good advice and ideas, based on the wisdom gained throughout her long life. However, grandchildren often only a have very partial view of the grandmother figure. This book is therefore a way of getting to know her better, because every page can be used to collect the thoughts, stories, experiences and scenes of family life that your grandmother would like to share, opening the drawers of her memory so as to leave the new generations of her family with her life story and teachings for the future. The blank pages of this book, somewhere between a scrapbook and a diary, will gradually be filled with the stories of her life, immortalizing the past and thereby providing a precious guide for facing the future. It will therefore become an historical memoir and, at the same time, a testimony to the importance of one's roots.

Family Tree

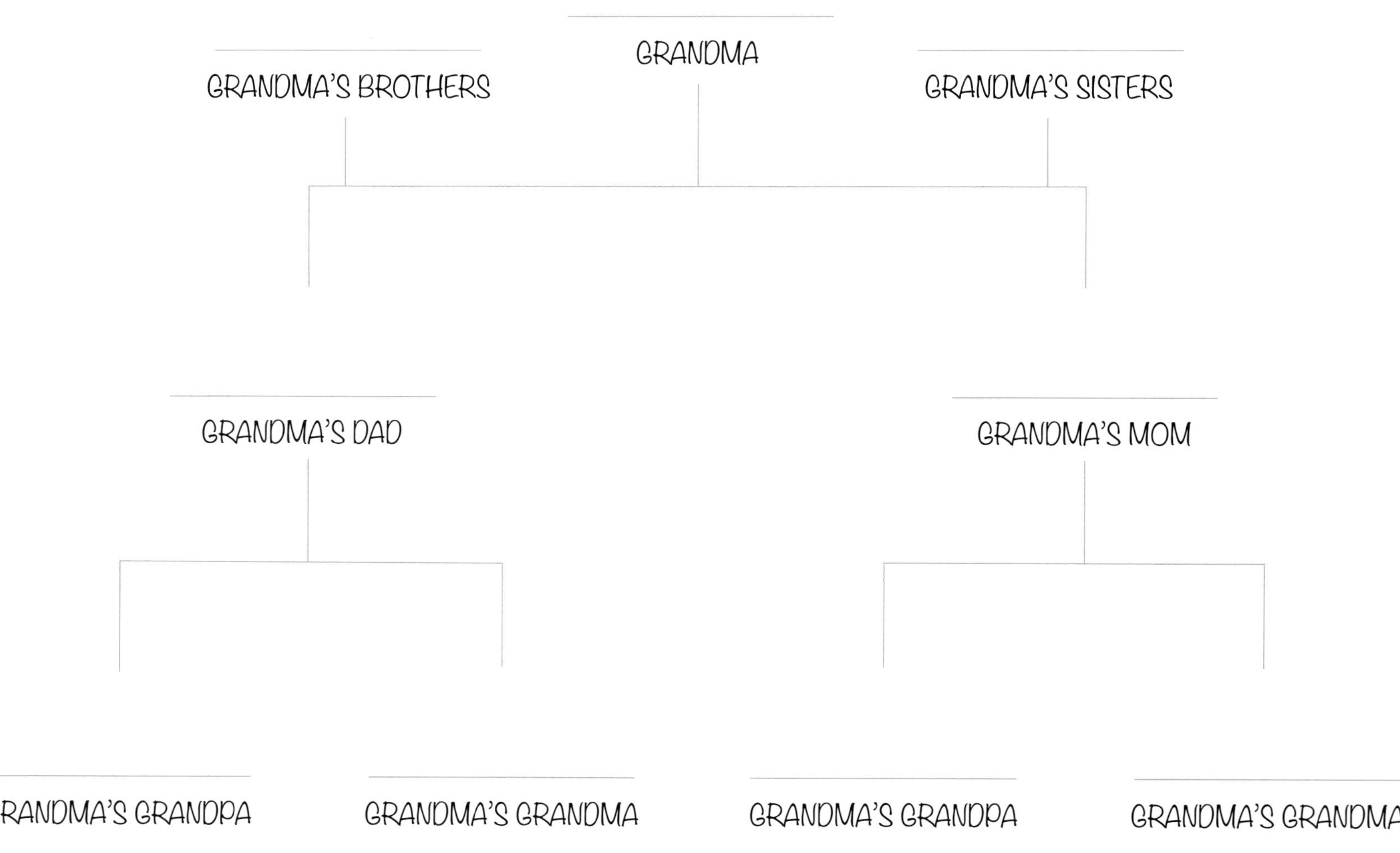

PHOTO

PHOTO

Grandma, Tell Me Your Story...

When and where were you born?

Tell me about your parents

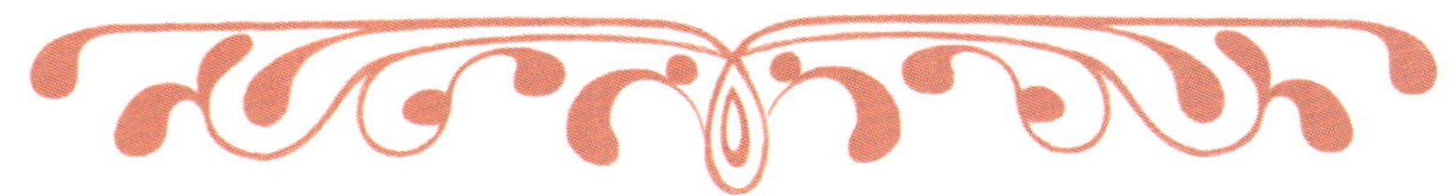

Tell me about your grandparents

Tell me about your brothers and sisters

What was your house like?

What did you used to do on holidays?

Do you remember a fairytale that you especially liked?

What was your favorite holiday?

Your Christmas

How did you celebrate Christmas?

Do you have any special memories?

PHOTO

What are your fondest memories of your Mom?

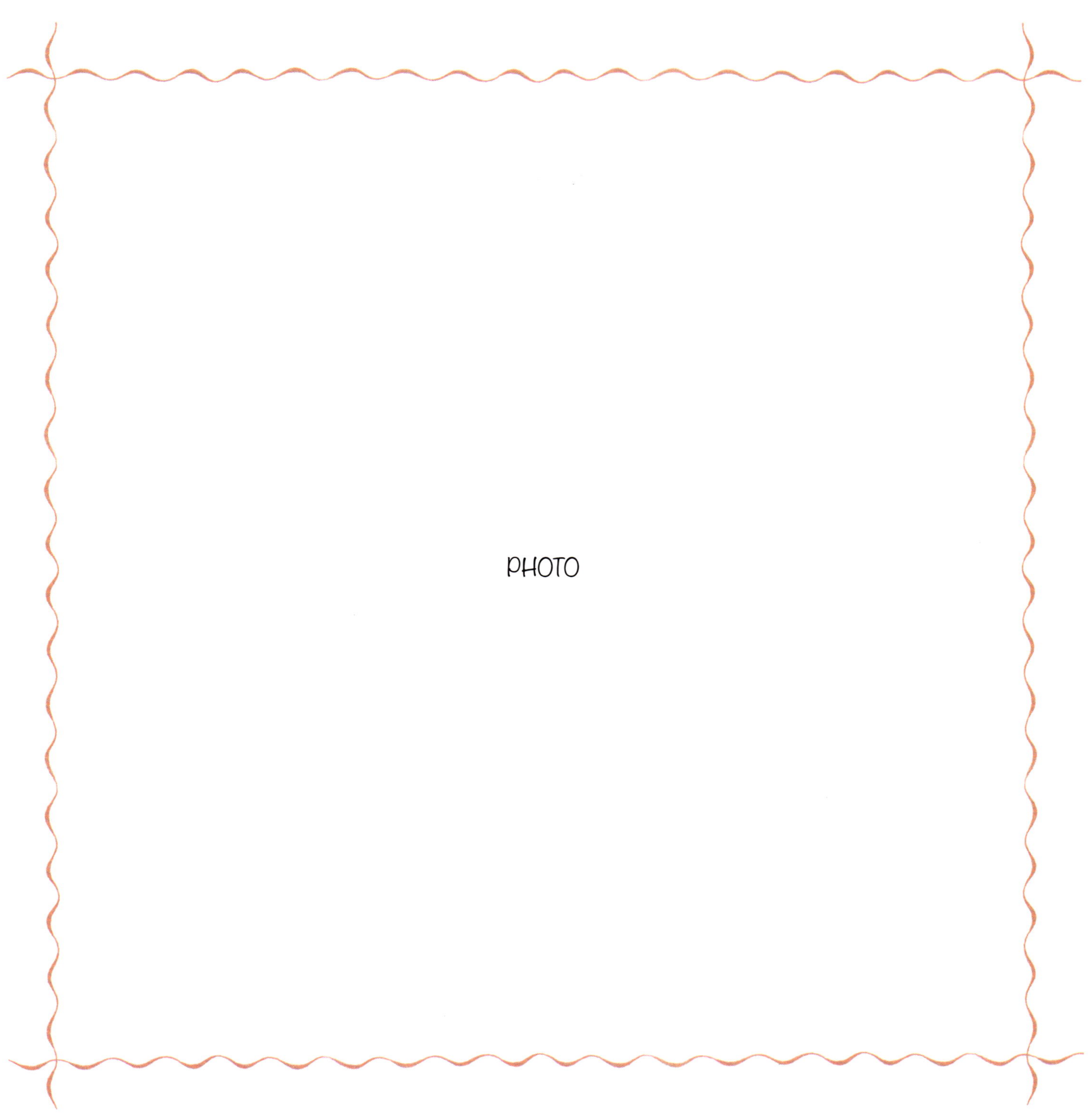
PHOTO

And of your Dad?

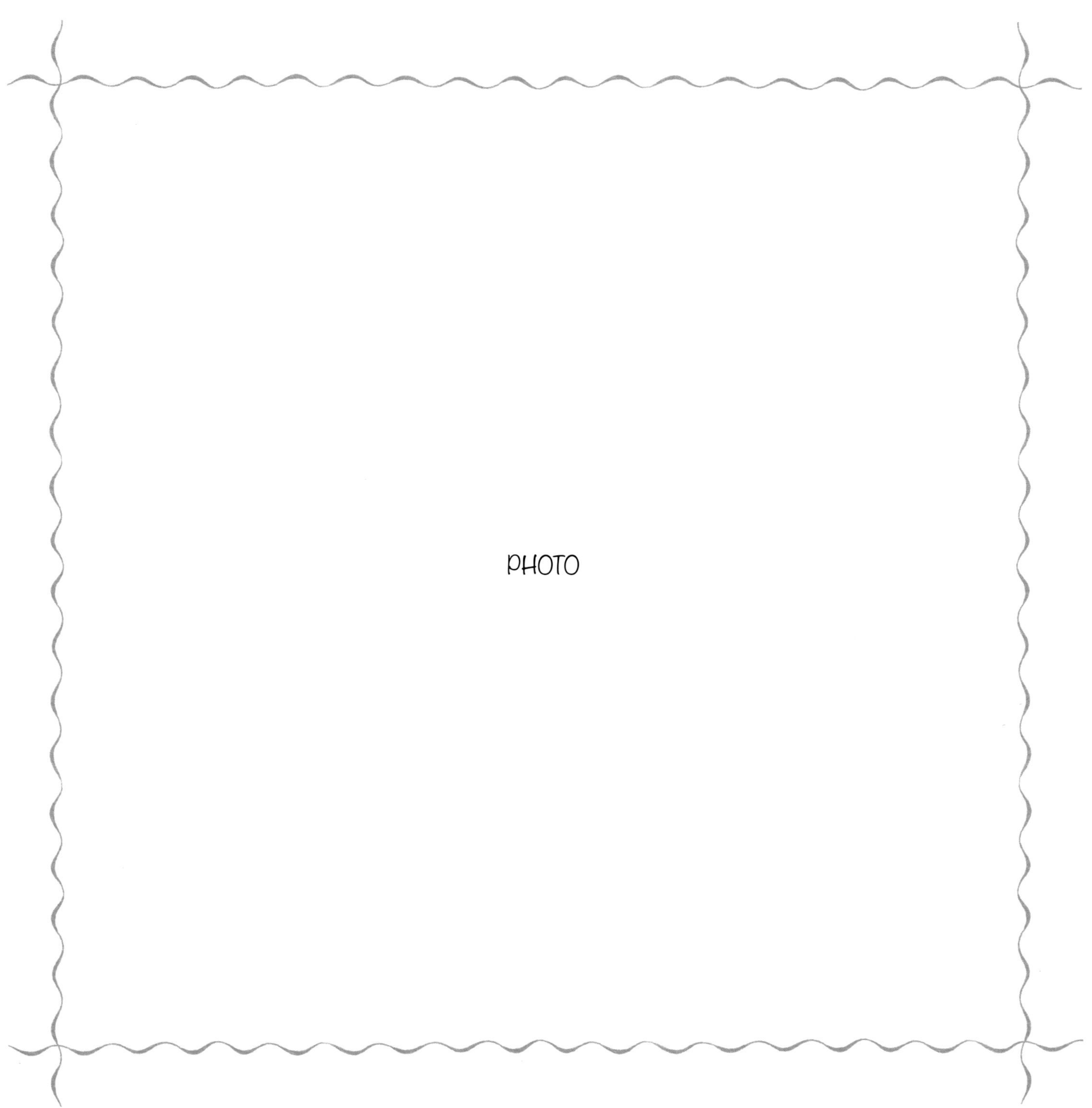
PHOTO

When You Were a Child...

What was your bedroom like?

Did you have a bedroom all to yourself?

What were your favorite games?

Who did you go to when you needed help?

PHOTO

PHOTO

Did you all eat together?

What were your favorite foods?

What did you do after dinner?

Did you help your Mom do housework?

Did you have special house cleaning chores?

What did you do on Sunday?

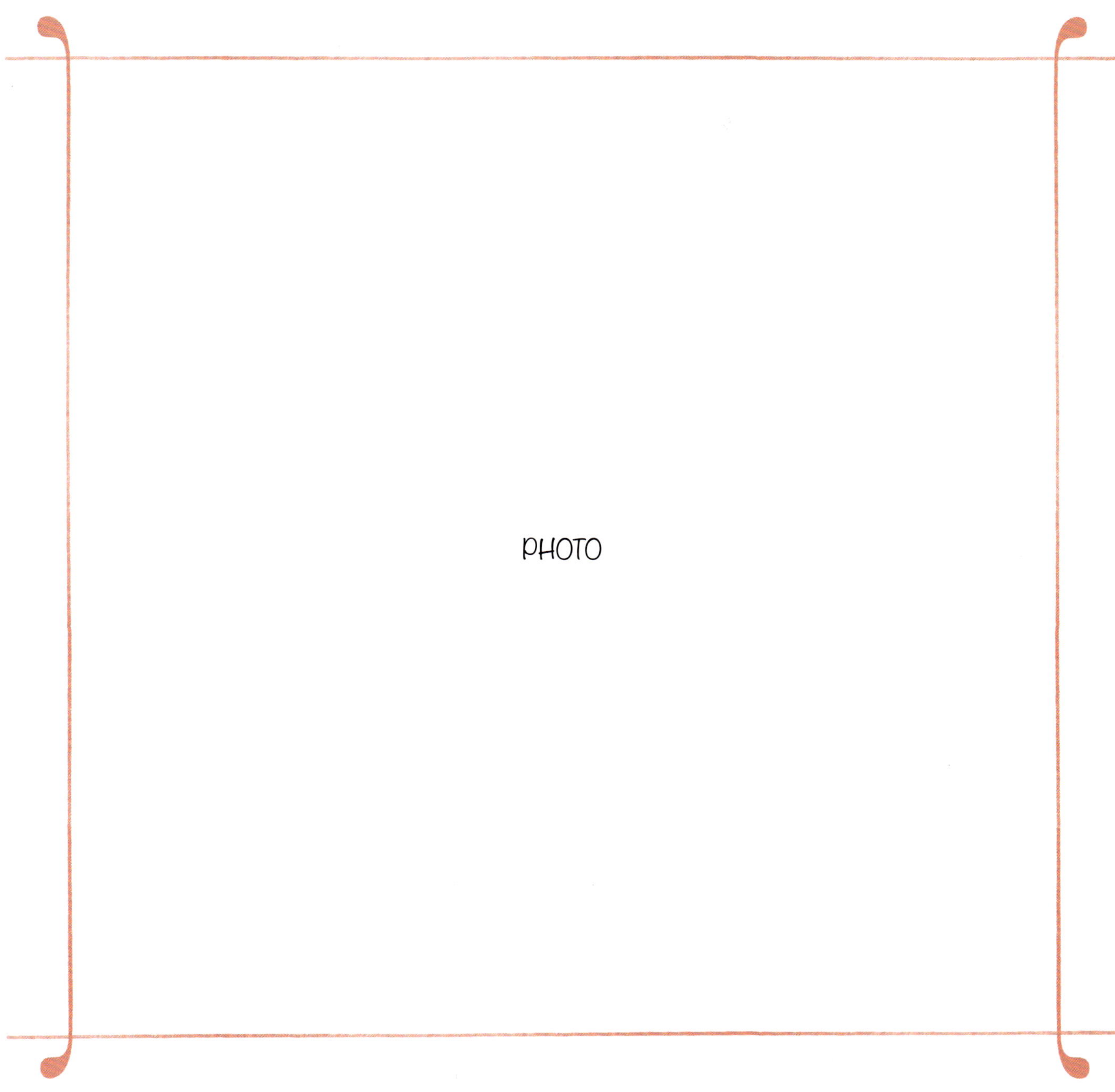
PHOTO

Who were your best friends?

What kind of games did you play?

Did you play any sports?

PHOTO

PHOTO

PHOTO

At School

Do you remember your first day at school?

What was your school like?

What was your teacher like?

How many classmates did you have and what were they like?

Who sat next to you?

PHOTO

What were your favorite subjects?

Who took you to school?

Which schools did you go to?

What period of your school life did you like most and why?

What were your dreams and aspirations after finishing school?

PHOTO

PHOTO

How did you spend your time during summer vacation?

PHOTO

Your Job

What was your first job after school? How old were you?

Did you change jobs often? Tell me about it!

When You Met Grandpa...

When and where did you meet grandpa?

How old were you?

What struck you about him?

What was it about him that made him special?

When did you introduce him to your friends?

What did they say?

What did you like doing together?

What did you talk about?

Did you have lots of friends?

When and how did he ask you to marry him?

PHOTO

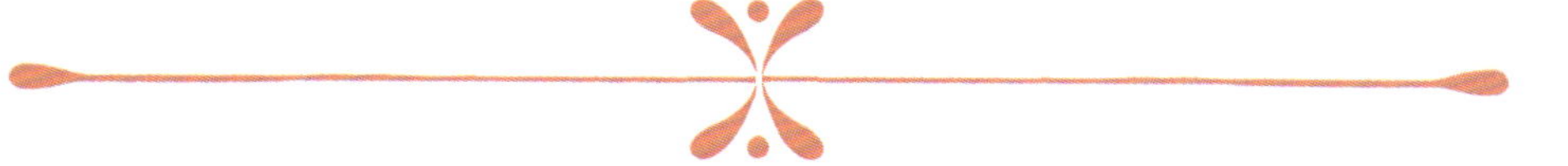

PHOTO

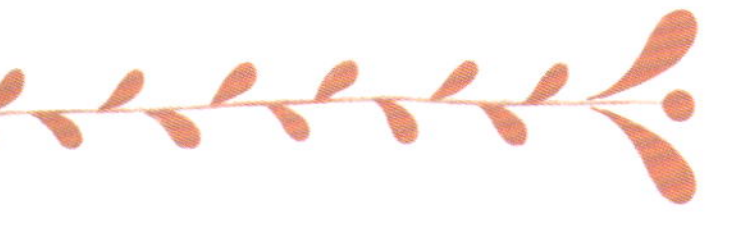

Your Wedding

When did you get married?

Tell me about your wedding

PHOTO

PHOTO

Where did you get married?

What was grandpa wearing?

Were you excited?

Who was there? What was the reception like?

PHOTO

PHOTO

Your Honeymoon

Where did you go on your honeymoon? What are your favorite memories?

PHOTO

PHOTO

The Start of a New Life...

Where did you go to live?

What was your house like?

When did you find out that you were going to be a mom?

How did Grandpa react when you told him?

How did your life together change?

What was Dad/Mom like when he/she was a child?

Who did he/she look like?

Photos of Dad/Mom when he/she was little

Tell me something else about Dad/Mom

Was he/she obedient?

How did he/she get to school?

Did he/she ever get into huge trouble?

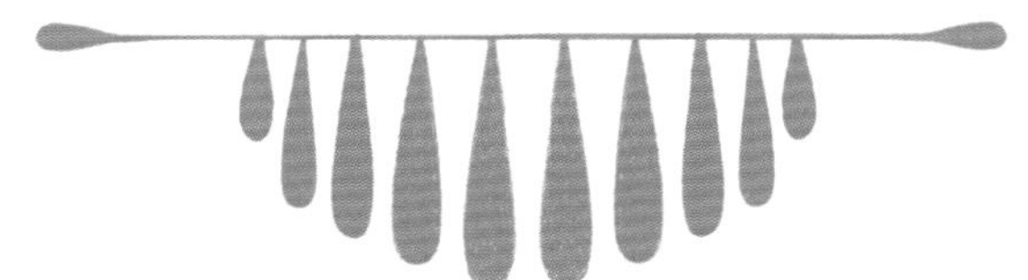

What are the happiest memories of your marriage?

What are the saddest memories?

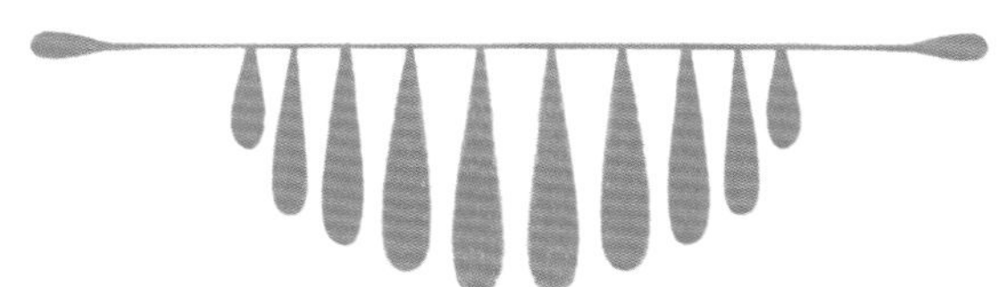

Did you celebrate holidays with your family?

Tell me about your vacations

PHOTO

PHOTO

...and Then I Arrived!

How did you feel about becoming a grandma?

What did you think when you saw me for the first time?

How did your life change?

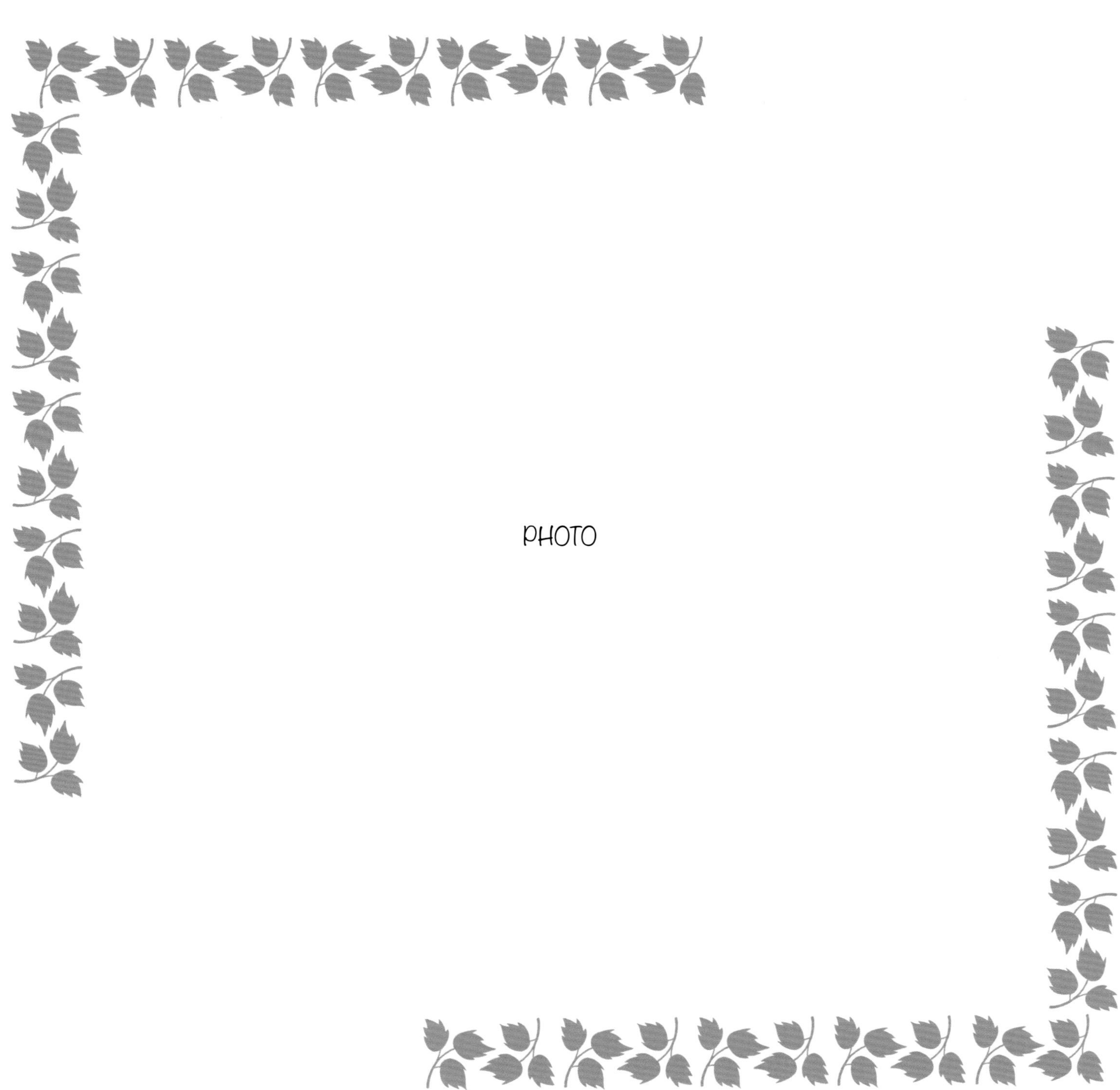
PHOTO

Which historical events do you remember during your lifetime?

Are you nostalgic about the olden days?

What do you think about the world today?

Do you have any regrets?

Would you change anything about your life?

What message would you like to leave for your family?

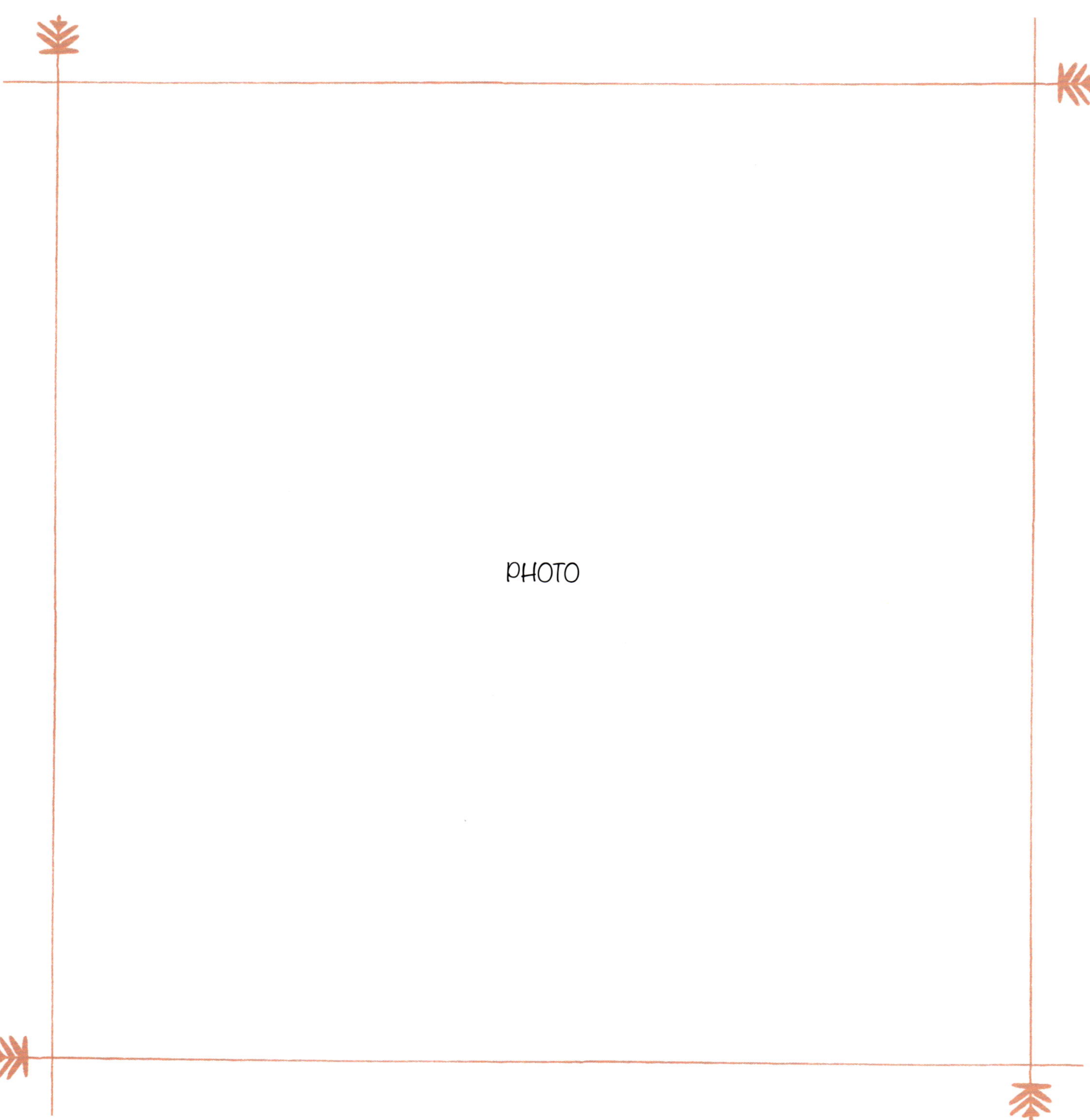
PHOTO

The Story Continues...

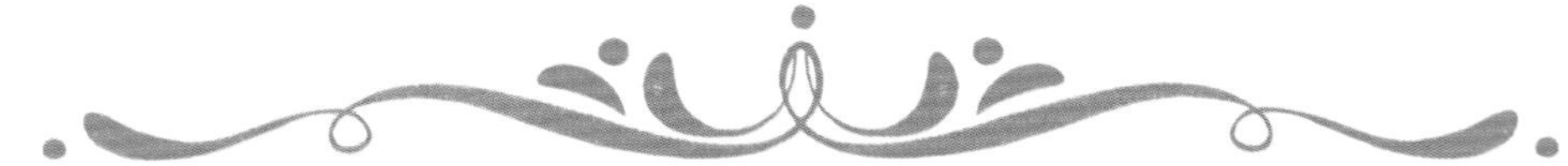

Illustrations

Francesca Rossi

Graphic Layout

Paola Piacco

Piazzale Luigi Cadorna, 6 - 20123 Milan, Italy
www.whitestar.it

Translation and Editing: TperTradurre s.r.l.

ISBN 978-88-544-2200-1
1 2 3 4 5 6   30 29 28 27 26

Printed in China